L'ALLEGRO

BY

JOHN MILTON

AND

WILLIAM BLAKE

MIRTH AND HER COMPANIONS

JOHN MILTON

L'ALLEGRO

WITH THE PAINTINGS BY
WILLIAM BLAKE

TOGETHER WITH
A NOTE UPON THE POEMS
BY W. P. TRENT

NEW YORK
THE HERITAGE PRESS

CONTENTS

A NOTE UPON THE POEMS

THE genesis of *L'Allegro* and *Il Penseroso*, perhaps the best known and most heartily admired of all Milton's compositions, is involved in considerable obscurity. They were not printed before 1645, and they do not exist for us in the celebrated bound volume of Milton's Mss. in the library of Trinity College, Cambridge, which contains the drafts of all the English poems written between 1633, probably, and 1645; we are therefore compelled, in the absence of other data, to rely upon inferences and internal evidence in determining their time and place of writing. The consensus of critical opinion gives 1631-34 as the time, and Horton as the place. Professor Masson assigns them to the latter half of 1632. There are, however, reasons to make one think that they should probably be placed earlier. The autumn of 1632 seems to be selected because Horton is usually assumed as the place of composition, and Milton went to reside there in July, 1632. He would naturally, argue the critics, be so impressed with the charms of the spot that he would turn to verse, and *L'Allegro* and *Il Penseroso*, and the *Song on May Morning*, which we have assigned to the Cambridge period, would be the outcome. But there is no proof that the poems were not written at Cambridge or in London as reminiscential tributes to the pleasures of a vacation spent in the country; and we know from a Latin prolusion or oration delivered, Masson thinks, either in the latter half of 1631 or the first part of 1632, that Milton spent "the last past summer . . . amid rural scenes and sequestered glades," and that he recalled "the supreme delight *he* had with the Muses." This vacation of 1631 may have been spent at Horton, for there is no proof that the elder Milton had not then acquired that property, and the young poet may have written his poems under the elms that so fascinated him, or have composed them on his return to college.

I incline to the former supposition. As we shall see, he was unquestionably supplied with hints for both his poems by Burton's *Anatomy*, surely a likely book for such a student as Milton to take with him on a vacation. Again, no one can read the *Prolusion on Earling Rising*, almost certainly Milton's, without thinking that much of the raw material of the two poems was in his brain and being expressed during his university life; nor can one read the other prolusions without seeing that Orpheus, the music of the spheres, and Platonism were much in his thoughts. Besides, about 1630, the date of the *Epitaph on Shakspere*, Milton was evidently to some extent occupied with his great forerunner, whose genius is honored in the poems, and a year later he was experimenting with the octosyllabic couplet in the *Epitaph on the Marchioness of Winchester*. Finally, it was about this time that he was seriously weighing the reasons *pro* and *con* with regard to his choice of a profession, and it might naturally occur to him to contrast in poetic form the pleasures of the more or less worldly and the more or less secluded, studious, and devoted life. He had made his choice by the autumn of 1632, and had therefore less cause for such poetical expression.

A minute analysis of the style and metre of the poems tends to confirm the view expressed above. It is obviously a transitional style when compared with that of the *Nativity Ode*, and other earlier pieces. Scriptural ideas and subjects are occupying his mind less and he has progressed toward a freer handling of his themes. He has become interested in contemporary English poetry, and while showing the influence of the classics, is not mastered by them. All this would indicate that the poems were written after 1631, though, as we have just seen, it is not unlikely that having in that year handled the octosyllabic couplet successfully, he should shortly be tempted to try it again. We thus have 1631 as a *terminus a quo;* 1633-1634, the years of *Arcades* and *Comus*, are a *terminus ad quem* for the following strictly metrical reasons. The lyrical portions of *Arcades* and *Comus* appear to be less spontaneous and more mature than *L'Allegro* and its companion poem. The metrical art displayed is more elaborate and self-conscious, and when one looks closer, as, for example, when one compares the invocation to Mirth in *L'Allegro* with the similar passage in *Comus* (ll. 102-122), one is struck with the fact that the verses of the anti-masque have lost the blithe sensuousness of the former poem, that thought is struggling with feeling, and that the lyric style of the poet is approaching its culmination in the elaborate and highly sustained art that has made *Lycidas* matchless. We conclude, therefore, that *L'Allegro* and *Il Penseroso* are nearer to the *Epitaph on the Marchioness of Winchester* than they are to *Arcades;* and if any one should argue that the mature sentiment of the poems and their vigorous expression indicate a later, not an earlier, date, it must suffice to reply that youth takes itself more seriously than age, and that there is no sentiment or thought in either poem that Milton might not well have had as a student at Cambridge.

It has been stated already that Milton was indebted for hints, if not for direct suggestion, to Burton's *Anatomy of Melancholy*. This famous book, the first edition of which appeared 1621, was prefaced by a poem entitled *The Author's Abstract of Melancholy*, Διαλογῶς, in which "Democritus Junior" analyzes his feelings in a way that foreshadows Milton's subsequent procedure. There are twelve stanzas of eight lines each, the last two verses of each stanza constituting a variable refrain, the measure being, however, the octosyllabic couplet. In one stanza the pleasures of a meditative man are given in a series of little pictures, while the next stanza presents the woes of the same personage when a fit of real melancholy is upon him. Milton could not have failed to be struck with the general effectiveness of the idea and its development, but his artist's instinct told him that this effectiveness would be enhanced if, instead of a dialogue in stanzas, he should write two distinct but companion poems, developed on parallel lines, in which the pleasures of a typically cheerful and a typically serious man should be described in pictures slightly more elaborate than those of Burton. He abandoned the too glaring contrast of joys and woes, and succeeded also in avoiding the occasional dropping into commonplace that mars the *Abstract of Melancholy*. But some pictures and even lines and phrases of the elder poem probably remained in his memory.

Another poem which may have influenced Milton is the song, "Hence, all you vain delights," in Fletcher's play, *The Nice Valour*. This play was not published until 1647, but it had been acted long before, and the song had almost certainly become known before *Il Penseroso* was written. Tradition assigns the lyric to Beaumont, but Mr. Bullen with more probability gives it to Fletcher. It is an exquisite expansion of the theme expressed in its closing verse, "Nothing's so dainty-sweet as lovely melancholy," and it is pleasant to believe that it may have given Milton a hint, although it can scarcely have had as much influence upon his verses as his own two poems plainly had upon a stanza of Collin's *The Passions*. There are naturally traces of other poets to be found in these productions of Milton's impressionable period, particularly of Joshua Sylvester, and to a less degree of Spenser, Browne, and Marlowe. Collins, too, was not the only eighteenth-century poet who had *L'Allegro* and *Il Penseroso* ringing through his head, as any one may see who will take the trouble to examine Dodsley's well-known collection. Even Pope was not above borrowing epithets from them, and Dyer's best poem, "Grongar Hill," would not have had its being without them. Matthew Green, Thomas Warton, John Hughes, who actually wrote a new conclusion for *Il Penseroso*, and other minor verse-writers were much affected by them, and Gray borrowed from them with the open boldness that always marks the appropriations of a true poet. But perhaps the best proof of their popularity during a century which is too sweepingly charged with inability to appreciate real poetry, is the fact that Handel set them to music. In our own century they have never lacked admirers, or failed to exert upon poets an easily detected influence. It may even be held with some show of reason that their popularity, leading to a fuller knowledge of Milton, paved the way for the remarkable renaissance of Spenser in the eighteenth and nineteenth centuries.

As their Italian titles imply, the subjects or speakers of Milton's verses are The Cheerful Man and The Thoughtful (Meditative) Man respectively. Our English adjectives do not quite adequately render the Italian they are intended to translate, which is perhaps the reason why Milton went abroad for his titles, since he had a striking warning before him in Burton's *Abstract* of the ambiguity attaching to such a word as "melancholy," which he might have used with one of his poems without exciting surprise. He has excited surprise with some modern critics through the fact that he wrote *Penseroso* instead of *Pensieroso*, but it has been seemingly shown that the form he used was correct and current when he wrote. His Italian titles, however, have not prevented much discussion as to the characters he intended to portray. Critics are quite unanimously of the opinion that *Il Penseroso* represents a man very like the Milton we know, but they are divided as to the kind of man typified by *L'Allegro*. One editor, Mr. Verity, goes so far as to say that Milton "must have felt that the character of *L'Allegro* might, with slight changes or additions, be made to typify the careless, pleasure-seeking spirit of the Cavaliers and Court; the spirit which he afterward figured in Comus and his followers, and condemned to destruction." If this view be correct, one is forced to conclude that Milton had more of the true dramatist's power of creating characters other than himself than he has generally been supposed to possess; and it requires us to conceive the more sprightly poem as forming a hard mechanical contrast to its companion, which is the reverse of poetical. On the other hand, Dr. Garnett maintains that the two poems "are complementary rather than contrary, and may be, in a sense, regarded as one poem, whose theme is the praise of the reasonable life." It is easy to agree with this view, especially as Burton's poem obviously suggested the idea of contrasting two well-marked moods of one individual character, rather than that of bringing into juxtaposition two radically different characters. *L'Allegro* may not be the Milton who meditated entering the Church and making his life a true poem, but he is rather the Milton who went to the theatre in his youth than the typical Cavalier of Charles's court. Cavaliers did not usually call for "sweet Liberty" but for sweet License, nor did they greatly hanker after "unreproved

14

pleasures." They were not particularly noted for their early rising; and if any one of them had watched the Bear out, in different pursuits from those of *Il Penseroso*, he would probably not have continued his morning walk after encountering the "milkmaid singing blithe."

Another point on which critics differ is, whether or not Milton intended to describe the events of a day of twenty-four hours. Some claim that he merely sketches the general tenor of the life of his characters; others that he represents the events of an ideal day. The antagonists ought to be satisfied with the assurance that he intended to do both the one thing and the other. The careful and sequential division of the day that is apparent in each poem (even if *Il Penseroso* does begin with the nightingale and the moon) cannot be accidental, nor can the grouping of events and natural sights belonging to different seasons of the year be the result of ignorance.

It is, probably, a fad of criticism to call as much attention as is now done to the fact that Milton was not so accurate or so penetrating an observer of nature as some of his successors, like Tennyson, have been. In the first place, neither here nor in *Paradise Lost* will Milton be found to be much of a sinner in this regard if he be compared with his predecessors and contemporaries. In the second place, it is by no means certain that minute and accurate observation of nature is essential to the equipment of a great poet. A genuine love of nature, a power to feel and impart something of her spirit, is doubtless essential; but as poetry on its pictorial side should be mainly suggestive, it is not yet clear that posterity will get more pleasure out of the elaborate and accurate pictures of some modern poets than out of the broadly true and suggestive, if sometimes inaccurate, pictures of Milton. It is not entirely unlikely that our recently developed love of detail-work has injured our sense for form, and that our grandchildren will take Matthew Arnold's advice and return to the Greeks—and Milton, in order to learn what the highest poetry really is like. Milton is nearer akin to Homer and Sophocles than he is to the modern naturalist or nature mystic, and it is well for English poetry that he is. He would probably have thought the picture of the sunbeams lying in the golden chamber, suggested by a few words in that exquisite fragment of Mimnermus beginning "Ἀξηταω πόλιν," more in keeping with the requirements of a rational poetics than nine-tenths of the purple descriptive passages in English poetry since the days of Wordsworth.

Yet if editors and critics have had their humors and fads, they have always ended by acknowledging the perennial charm of these poems. And the mass of readers has paid its highest tribute of culling many a phrase and verse for quotation.

L' ALLEGRO

BY

JOHN MILTON
&
WILLIAM BLAKE

L'ALLEGRO

Hence loathèd Melancholy,

  Of Cerberus and blackest Midnight born,

In Stygian Cave forlorn

  'Mongst horrid shapes, and shrieks, and sights unholy!

Find out some uncouth cell,

  Where brooding Darkness spreads his jealous wings,

And the night-Raven sings;

  There under Ebon shades, and low-browed Rocks,

As ragged as thy Locks,

  In dark Cimmerian desert ever dwell.

But come, thou Goddess fair and free,

In Heaven yclept Euphrosyne,

And by men, heart-easing Mirth,

Whom lovely Venus, at a birth,

With two sister Graces more,

To Ivy-crownèd Bacchus bore;

Or whether (as some Sager sing)

The Frolic Wind that breathes the Spring,

Zephir with Aurora playing,

As he met her once a-Maying,

There, on Beds of Violets blue,

And fresh-blown Roses washed in dew,

Filled her with thee, a daughter fair,

So buxom, blithe, and debonair.

　　Haste thee, Nymph, and bring with thee

Jest and youthful Jollity,

Quips and Cranks, and wanton Wiles,

Nods, and Becks, and Wreathèd Smiles,

Such as hang on Hebe's cheek,

And love to live in dimple sleek;

Sport that wrinkled Care derides,

And Laughter holding both his sides.

Come, and trip it as ye go

On the light fantastic toe,

And in thy right hand lead with thee,

The Mountain Nymph, sweet Liberty;

And if I give thee honor due,

Mirth, admit me of thy crew

To live with her, and live with thee,

In unprovèd pleasures free;

To hear the Lark begin his flight,

And, singing, startle the dull night,

From his watch-tower in the skies,

Till the dappled dawn doth rise;

Then to come in spite of sorrow,

And at my window bid good-morrow,

Through the Sweet-Briar, or the Vine,

Or the twisted Eglantine.

While the Cock, with lively din,

NIGHT STARTLED BY THE LARK

Scatters the rear of darkness thin,

And to the stack, or the Barn-door,

Stoutly struts his Dames before,

Oft listening how the Hounds and horn

Clearly rouse the slumbering morn,

From the side of some Hoar Hill,

Through the high wood echoing shrill.

Some time walking not unseen

By Hedge-row Elms, on Hillocks green,

Right against the Eastern gate,

Where the great Sun begins his state,

Robed in flames, and Amber light,

The clouds in thousand Liveries dight.

While the Plowman, near at hand,

Whistles o'er the Furrowed Land,

And the Milkmaid singeth blithe,

And the Mower whets his scythe,

And every Shepherd tells his tale

Under the Hawthorn in the dale.

Straight mine eye hath caught new pleasures

Whilst the Landscape round it measures,

Russet Lawns, and Fallows Gray,

Where the nibbling flocks do stray,

Mountains on whose barren breast

The laboring clouds do often rest:

Meadows trim with Daisies pied,

THE GREAT SUN

Shallow Brooks, and Rivers wide.

Towers, and Battlements it sees

Bosomed high in tufted Trees,

Where perhaps some beauty lies,

The Cynosure of neighboring eyes.

Hard by a Cottage chimney smokes,

From betwixt two aged Oaks,

Where Corydon and Thyrsis met,

Are at their savory dinner set

Of Herbs, and other Country Messes,

Which the neat-handed Phillis dresses;

And then in haste her Bower she leaves,

With Thestylis to bind the Sheaves;

Or, if the earlier season lead,

To the tanned Haycock in the Mead.

Sometimes with secure delight

The upland Hamlets will invite,

When the merry Bells ring round,

And the jocund rebecks sound

To many a youth, and many a maid,

Dancing in the Chequered shade;

And young and old come forth to play

On a Sunshine Holyday,

Till the live-long day-light fail;

Then to the Spicy Nut-brown Ale,

With stories told of many a feat,

THE SUNSHINE HOLIDAY

How Faery Mab the junkets eat.

She was pinched, and pulled she said;

And he, by Friar's Lantern led,

Tells how the drudging Goblin sweat,

To earn his Cream-bowl duly set,

When in one night, ere glimpse of morn,

His shadowy Flail hath threshed the Corn

That ten day-laborers could not end,

Then lies him down, the lubber fiend,

And stretched out all the Chimney's length,

Basks at the fire his hairy strength;

And Crop-full out of doors he flings,

Ere the first Cock his Matin rings.

Thus done the Tales, to bed they creep,

By whispering Winds soon lulled asleep.

   Towered Cities please us then,

And the busy hum of men,

Where throngs of Knights and Barons bold,

In weeds of Peace high triumphs hold,

With store of Ladies, whose bright eyes

Rain influence, and judge the prize

Of Wit, or Arms, while both contend

To win her Grace, whom all commend.

There let Hymen oft appear

In Saffron robe, with Taper clear,

And pomp, and feast, and revelry,

THE STORIES OF CORYDON AND THYRSIS

With mask, and antique Pageantry,

Such sights as youthful Poets dream

On Summer eves by haunted stream.

Then to the well-trod stage anon,

If Jonson's learnèd Sock be on,

Or sweetest Shakespeare, Fancy's child,

Warble his native Wood-notes wild;

And ever, against eating Cares,

Lap me in soft Lydian Airs,

Married to immortal verse

Such as the meeting soul may pierce

In notes, with many a winding bout

Of linkèd sweetness long drawn out,

With wanton heed, and giddy cunning,

The melting voice through mazes running;

Untwisting all the chains that tie

The hidden soul of harmony;

That Orpheus' self may heave his head

From golden slumber on a bed

Of heaped Elysian flowers, and hear

Such strains as would have won the ear

Of Pluto, to have quite set free

His half-regained Eurydice.

These delights, if thou canst give,

Mirth, with thee I mean to live.

THE YOUNG POET'S DREAM

BLAKE'S INSCRIPTIONS ON HIS PAINTINGS

MIRTH AND HER COMPANIONS

These personifications are all brought together in the First design Surrounding the Principal Figure which is Mirth herself.

NIGHT STARTLED BY THE LARK

The Lark is an Angel on the Wing. Dull Night starts from his Watch Tower on a Cloud. The Dawn with her Dappled Horses arises above the Earth. The Earth beneath awakes at the Lark's Voice.

THE GREAT SUN

The Great Sun is represented clothed in Flames, Surrounded by the Clouds in their Liveries, in their various Offices at the Eastern Gate; beneath, in Small Figures, Milton walking by Elms on Hillocks green, The Plowman, The Milkmaid, The Mower whetting his Scythe, and The Shepherd and his Lass under a Hawthorn in the Dale.

THE SUNSHINE HOLIDAY

In this design is Introduced,

> *Mountains on whose barren breast*
> *The labouring clouds do often rest.*

Mountains, Clouds, Rivers, Trees appear Humanized on the Sunshine Holiday. The Church Steeple with its merry bells. The Clouds arise from the bosoms of Mountains, While Two Angels sound their Trumpets in the Heavens to announce the Sunshine Holiday.

THE STORIES OF CORYDON AND THYRSIS

The Goblin crop full flings out of doors from his Laborious task dropping his Flail & Cream bowl, yawning & stretching, vanishes into the Sky, in which is seen Queen Mab Eating the Junkets. The Sports of the Fairies are seen thro' the Cottage where "She" lays in Bed, 'pinch'd & pull'd' by Fairies as they dance on the Bed, the Ceiling & the Floor, & a Ghost pulls the Bed Clothes at her Feet. "He" is seen following the Friar's Lantern towards the Convent.

THE YOUNG POET'S DREAM

The Youthful Poet, sleeping on a bank by the Haunted Stream by Sun Set, sees in his dream the more bright Sun of Imagination under the auspices of Shakespeare & Johnson [Jonson], in which is Hymen at a Marriage & the Antique Pageantry attending it.

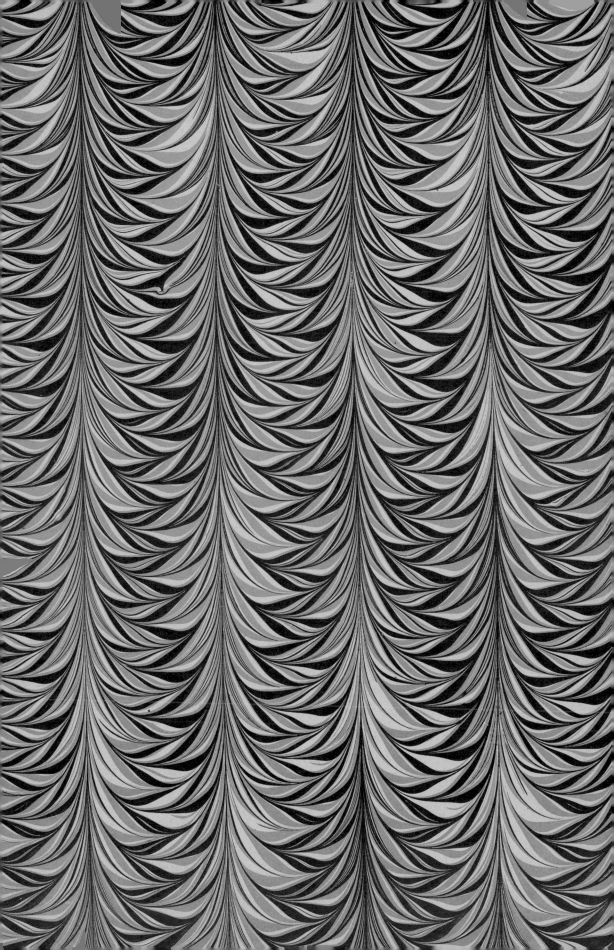

IL PENSEROSO

BY

JOHN MILTON

AND

WILLIAM BLAKE

MELANCHOLY AND HER COMPANIONS

JOHN MILTON

IL PENSEROSO

WITH THE PAINTINGS BY
WILLIAM BLAKE

TOGETHER WITH
A NOTE UPON THE PAINTINGS BY
CHAUNCEY BREWSTER TINKER

NEW YORK
THE HERITAGE PRESS

CONTENTS

A NOTE UPON THE PAINTINGS

THE Pierpont Morgan Library has recently, through the generosity of its newly formed group of Fellows, come into possession of William Blake's twelve illustrations in watercolor for Milton's two "minor poems," *L'Allegro* and *Il Penseroso*. Although these were never engraved or reproduced in any way by the artist, they have long been known to exist, and indeed have been used as illustrations (in collotype) in the Nonesuch edition of Milton's English poems, enriched with notes by Mr. Geoffrey Keynes. The full series, six drawings for *L'Allegro* and six for *Il Penseroso*, was first reproduced in color by Mr. Adrian Van Sinderen in his *Blake, the Mystic Genius*.

The watercolors were accompanied, apparently from the beginning, by twelve sheets of writing in Blake's hand, carrying the lines from the poem which the artist has illustrated, together with some notes mentioning details which are to be found in the pictures. These, too, have been seen and used before, with the exception of the original titles which Blake gave to the pictures. The titles, hitherto overlooked and replaced by others less accurate, are on the verso of the sheets, and have now been found and deciphered as follows: for *L'Allegro: Mirth; The Lark; The Sun at His Eastern Gate; A Sunshine Holiday; The Goblin; The Youthful Poet's Dream;* for *Il Penseroso:Melancholy; The Wandering Moon; The Spirit of Plato; The Sun in His Wrath; Mysterious Dream; Milton, Old Age.* These titles are simpler and somewhat more natural than those devised by W. M. Rossetti, and used by succeeding critics.

The watercolors are on sheets measuring about 6⅜ by 4⅞ inches, and each is signed *W. Blake inv.* The watermark "M & J Lay 1816" is found in the paper on which the designs are painted, and seems therefore to fix a date subsequent to which the watercolors were made. The artist was perhaps entering upon the period of his great labors which were to result in the illustrations for the *Book of Job*, for *Paradise Lost* and for Dante's *Divine Comedy.*

Milton's *L'Allegro* and *Il Penseroso* are two contrasted and highly personal *études* to which he gave two rather inaccurate Italian titles. Blake gave them the still more confusing titles *Mirth* and *Melancholy.* The scenes of the first six are not in every case mirthful, and the lovely figure of *Melancholy* never

8

suggests gloom or depression, or any other mood commonly associated with that word.

Blake's twelve illustrations, though wanting the grotesqueness and sublimity associated with his name, are found on examination to have a strangeness and an esoteric quality quite their own. Indeed students and interpreters of the symbols used by Blake—by no means always in agreement with one another—will have much to say about the tiny details which fill to overflowing the scenes set before us. The drawings are of course never merely illustrative of what the artist found in the brief and flashing scenes of the two companion poems. Here, as elsewhere, he uses the poems to enable him to give expression to his own philosophy of existence, and to his somewhat novel view of the relation of the sexes. But though he departs often enough from the spirit of his Miltonic originals he does not pass by the gaiety of the two opening pictures of the *Allegro* group or the deepening sense of solemnity as the whole series progresses. These aspects of Blake's work can be and should be enjoyed by those who feel a natural delight in the man's vivid and blending colors and in the dreamlike scenes which he has the power to call up before us.

One aspect of Blake's world of the imagination as seen by the ordinary observer like myself may perhaps be described.

It is a kind of freedom from stifling material conditions. As the twelve watercolors are examined in turn, we never have the sense of being "shut in," whether in the gaiety of the Elizabethan theatre of *L'Allegro* or the "studious cloister's pale" of *Il Penseroso*. We have an abiding sense of being in the open—almost, one might say, *"en plein air,"* if it were not that our sight is extended beyond our mortal ken. The human beings, no less than the (more important) fairies, spirits, emanations and allegorical figures that fill the scene, are not restricted by the "ordinary" boundaries of life or limited by laws falsely considered natural.

The artist's first interest is not in human beings, their pastoral occupations and humble pleasures. Milton speaks of Corydon and Thyrsis as "at their savoury dinner set Of herbs and other country messes, Which the neat-handed Phillis dresses"; Blake mentions them also, but reduces all such creatures—the laboring ploughman, the merry milkmaid, and even woods and trees—to "small figures," as he phrases it. They are indeed all but invisible, as may be shown from his third picture in the *Allegro* series, *The Sun at His Eastern Gate*. It is the life-giving and imperial god that delights the painter, because he is a potent force, arising in splendor, attended by his suitors, clouds "in their liveries," with hosts of winged beings, ministering spirits, no doubt, bringers of good things to men at dawn. Beauteous is the princely Sun at his appearing, but dire is his smiting wrath at noonday.

Again, in *The Goblin* drawing, we have the same impression of conditions transcended. There is, to be sure, a bedroom visible, with fairies dancing on the floor, the coverlet of the bed and, astonishingly, on the ceiling, while a ghost (Blake assures us that it is a ghost) stands at the foot of the bed, tormenting the poor occupant.

But all this is only a *glimpse*. What is going on in the air around is more important. Say what you may of details, it is the Goblin who fills the scene. In the *poem* the fiend, after his kindly miracle, is described as "stretched out all the chimney's length," basking in front of the fire, his labors ended. Thus Milton suggests a pleasant interior scene, somewhat in the Dutch manner; but Blake will have none of it. The stupendous Goblin, yawning and stretching with weariness, drops the flail with which he has done his work and the cream-bowl which was his reward, and begins his disappearance into thin air. Far above in the sky, Fairy Mab is shown eating the junkets. On earth some belated traveler follows "the Friar's Lantern towards the Convent." Plainly there is mischief abroad, and the Powers of the Air are astir.

The last picture in the *Allegro* group is, appropriately, *The Youthful Poet's Dream*, which Blake apparently regards as the climax of his work thus far. The boy Milton slumbers upon a bank under a tree; beside him there is a large unwritten folio volume, while his right hand holds a pen and his left is slightly raised as though responsive, even in sleep, to the dream above his head. The sun, which has been shown before in his glory, is now sinking, and the flowing stream and the cool air are already haunted by fairylike beings. But there is a greater and a supreme Power at work upon the youthful poet—the "Sun of Imagination" which dwarfs the setting sun, large as that is, and which appears as a vast sphere above the dreamer's head while Shakespeare and Ben Jonson, as the masters of masque and antique pageantry, preside over it, on either hand. And here there enters the series the theme of Hymen ("with saffron robe and taper clear") which, even if one fully understood it, could hardly be translated into words. Let the reader instruct himself by searching out the number of embracing lovers which may be found here and elsewhere in the series. To follow the artist's lead in such a way is more remunerative than the scrupulous acceptance of commentators' explanations.

Melancholy is, as I have said, erroneously named, for her sweet and solemn figure is attended by the maidens "Peace" and "Quiet," and "Leisure," the lover of trim gardens. To the right and left of her head are the silent figure of "Night," soothed by the nightingale's song, and the "New Moon" checking her dragon-team above the oak. *Melancholy* is, in truth, none other than "Wisdom's best Nurse," "Contemplation." Beside her is "Spare Fast" (apt personification of a poet!), who lifts his eyes to a vision of the circling Muses above his head, even as she herself raises her own to the flaming cherub who guides the fiery wheels of the Throne of God. In color, composition and lucidity, this is certainly among the loveliest of the pictures.

As Milton's preference was for *Il Penseroso*, so, I think, was Blake's. In the last five of the drawings he introduces Milton himself as a principal figure; and in one of them (the second, or *The Wandering Moon*) he attempts to depict the same setting that Milton uses when listening to the sullen toll of the curfew, borne across some wide-watered shore—a passage reminiscent of the *squilla di lontano* in Dante's *Purgatorio* (canto VIII).

But here we must not go astray. Blake was never greatly interested in pure landscape. He paints no soft nocturne. He does, it is true, give us a pleasant glimpse of the wide-watered shore, with a church-tower in the middle distance, and the Moon high in heaven. But Cynthia is no serene goddess, only a short-skirted fay, who appears directly before the eyes of John Milton, student at Christ's College, Cambridge, in long robe and mortarboard with pompon. This is hardly Romanticism. Here is no solemn ode to Evening. Blake's moon is vivid enough, and behind her are the radiant emblems by which she is known; but Blake has made it difficult to think of her as wandering disconsolate along heaven's pathless way, for we do not easily detect any trace of terror about her. We must re-read the artist's picture until we find the meaning which he tells us is there.

Milton's studies at Cambridge are shown us in the next drawing, entitled *The Spirit of Plato*. Here the young student, meditating upon an open volume, is confronted by the shade of the great Greek philosopher, and the Platonic heaven (according to Blake) is opened before him in a splendid confusion of classical detail which the artist has spared no pains in elaborating. The four Elements; the three Destinies; and the spheres of Venus, Mars and Jupiter are revealed in a vast scene of light, color line and symbol.

"Melancholy" has of course no part in this scene, and, in fact, appears but once again in the series, when, in the fourth picture, she leads the poet through the fierce shafts of the Sun in his mid-day wrath towards the cool shades of a quiet grove.

As the two of them pass along their way, Blake bids us notice that the trees are under the domination of insects raised by the Sun's heat—a surprising contrast to the majesty of *The Sun at His Eastern Gate*.

This domination, however, does not extend to the scene depicted in the fifth watercolor, where the dream-imagery is again employed. The poet slumbering upon the ground is surrounded by six small fairylike figures "hovering on the air" with instruments of music. Here the *dominant* figure is the personification of "Sleep" (or rather of the inspiration conveyed in sleep)—a vast spirit descending from heaven, with the "strange, mysterious dream" upon his enormous pinions. The mystery of course must remain a mystery still; but Blake speaks of it as a process of unveiling, with "Scrolls and Nets and Webs, unfolded by Spirits in the Air and in the Brook." The sweep and the splendor of this conception of divine inspiration, personified and visible before us, are a fine example of Blake's transcendent genius.

In the final scene of all, Milton is represented as in old age. Seated in his "mossy cell," with open book and lighted lamp, he is still lost in contemplation of the heavens, whence power had descended long since upon him. There is no hint of blindness, which Blake apparently refuses to recognize. Whether the poet rightly "spells" the constellations over his head is a matter of no great importance. Above belted Orion, with lifted sword, we behold four signs of the zodiac, the Ram, the Bull, Gemini and the Crab, which must be taken to indicate spring and early summer; for on earth all is bursting into life. At the poet's side the rose and the lily take visible human form, and the whole of nature is "commercing with the skies." The poet's arms are opened wide in rapt wonder at the glory of the universe, and his lips are parted as he breaks into prophetic song.

IL PENSEROSO

BY

JOHN MILTON
&
WILLIAM BLAKE

IL PENSEROSO

Hence vain deluding Joys,

   The brood of Folly without father bred!

How little you bestead,

   Or fill the fixèd mind with all your toys;

Dwell in some idle brain,

   And fancies fond with gaudy shapes possess,

As thick and numberless

   As the gay motes that people the sun-beams,

Or likest hovering dreams

   The fickle Pensioners of Morpheus' train.

But hail, thou Goddess, sage and holy,

Hail, divinest Melancholy!

Whose Saintly visage is too bright

To hit the sense of human sight;

And therefore to our weaker view,

O'er-laid with black, staid Wisdom's hue.

Black, but such as in esteem,

Prince Memnon's sister might beseem,

Or that Starred Ethiope Queen that strove

To set her beauty's praise above

The Sea Nymphs, and their powers offended.

Yet thou art higher far descended

Thee bright-haired Vesta long of yore,

MILTON'S VISION OF THE MOON

To solitary Saturn bore;

His daughter she (in Saturn's reign,

Such mixture was not held a stain).

Oft in glimmering Bowers, and glades

He met her, and in secret shades

Of woody Ida's inmost grove,

Whilst yet there was no fear of Jove.

Come, pensive Nun, devout and pure,

Sober, steadfast, and demure,

All in a robe of darkest grain,

Flowing with majestic train,

And sable stole of Cypress Lawn,

Over thy decent shoulders drawn.

Come, but keep thy wonted state,

With even step, and musing gait,

And looks commercing with the skies,

Thy rapt soul sitting in thine eyes:

There, held in holy passion still,

Forget thy self to Marble, till

With a sad Leaden downward cast,

Thou fix them on the earth as fast.

And join with thee calm Peace, and Quiet,

Spare Fast, that oft with gods doth diet,

And hears the Muses in a ring,

Aye round about Jove's Altar sing.

And add to these retired Leisure,

MILTON AND THE SPIRIT OF PLATO

That in trim Gardens takes his pleasure;

But first, and chiefest, with thee bring,

Him that yon soars on golden wing,

Guiding the fiery-wheeled throne,

The Cherub Contemplation,

And the mute Silence hist along,

'Less Philomel will deign a Song,

In her sweetest, saddest plight,

Smoothing the rugged brow of Night,

While Cynthia checks her Dragon yoke,

Gently o'er th' accustomed Oak;

Sweet Bird, that shunn'st the noise of folly,

Most musical, most melancholy!

Thee, Chauntress, oft the Woods among,

I woo to hear thy even-song;

And missing thee, I walk unseen

On the dry smooth-shaven Green,

To behold the wandering Moon,

Riding near her highest noon,

Like one that had been led astray

Through the Heaven's wide pathless way;

And oft, as if her head she bowed,

Stooping through a fleecy cloud.

Oft on a Plat of rising ground,

I hear the far-off Curfew sound,

Over some wide-watered shore,

MILTON LED BY MELANCHOLY

Swinging slow with sullen roar;

Or if the Air will not permit,

Some still removèd place will fit,

Where glowing Embers through the room

Teach light to counterfeit a gloom,

Far from all resort of mirth,

Save the Cricket on the hearth,

Or the Bellman's drowsy charm,

To bless the doors from nightly harm

Or let my Lamp, at midnight hour,

Be seen in some high lonely Tower,

Where I may oft out-watch the Bear,

With thrice great Hermes, or unsphere

The spirit of Plato to unfold

What Worlds, or what vast Regions hold

The immortal mind that hath forsook

Her mansion in this fleshly nook

And of those Daemons that are found

In fire, air, flood, or under ground,

Whose power hath a true consent

With Planet, or with Element.

Some time let Gorgeous Tragedy

In Sceptered Pall come sweeping by,

Presenting Thebes, or Pelops' line,

Or the tale of Troy divine,

Or what (though rare) of later age,

MILTON'S DREAM

VILLON'S DREAM.

Ennoblèd hath the Buskined stage.

But, O sad Virgin, that thy power

Might raise Musaeus from his bower,

Or bid the soul of Orpheus sing

Such notes as, warbled to the string,

Drew Iron tears down Pluto's cheek,

And made Hell grant what Love did seek.

Or call up him that left half told

The story of Cambuscan bold,

Of Camball, and of Algarsife,

And who had Canace to wife,

That owned the virtuous Ring and Glass,

And of the wondrous Horse of Brass,

On which the Tartar King did ride;

And if aught else great Bards beside,

In sage and solemn tunes have sung,

Of Tourneys and of Trophies hung;

Of Forest, and enchantments drear,

Where more is meant than meets the ear.

Thus, Night, oft see me in thy pale career,

Till civil-suited Morn appear,

Not tricked and frounced as she was wont,

With the Attic Boy to hunt,

But Kerchiefed in a comely Cloud,

While rocking Winds are Piping loud,

Or ushered with a shower still,

THE PEACEFUL HERMITAGE

When the gust hath blown his fill,

Ending on the rustling Leaves,

With minute-drops from off the Eaves.

And when the Sun begins to fling

His flaring beams, me, Goddess, bring

To archèd walks of twilight groves,

And shadows brown, that Sylvan loves,

Of Pine, or monumental Oak,

Where the rude Ax with heavèd stroke,

Was never heard the Nymphs to daunt,

Or fright them from their hallowed haunt.

There in close covert by some Brook,

Where no profaner eye may look,

Hide me from Day's garish eye,

While the Bee with Honied thigh,

That at her flowery work doth sing,

And the Waters murmuring

With such consort as they keep,

Entice the dewy-feathered Sleep;

And let some strange mysterious dream,

Wave at his Wings, in Airy stream

Of lively portraiture displayed,

Softly on my eye-lids laid.

And as I wake, sweet music breathe

Above, about, or underneath,

Sent by some Spirit to mortals good,

Or th' unseen Genius of the Wood.

But let my due feet never fail,

To walk the studious Cloister's pale,

And love the high embowèd Roof,

With antique Pillars massy proof.

And storied Windows richly dight,

Casting a dim religious light.

There let the pealing Organ blow,

To the full voiced choir below,

In Service high, and Anthems clear,

As may with sweetness, through mine ear,

Dissolve me into ecstasies,

And bring all Heaven before mine eyes.

And may at last my weary age

Find out the peaceful hermitage,

The Hairy Gown and Mossy Cell,

Where I may sit and rightly spell

Of every Star that Heaven doth shew,

And every Herb that sips the dew;

Till old experience do attain

To something like Prophetic strain.

These pleasures, Melancholy, give,

And I with thee will choose to live.

BLAKE'S INSCRIPTIONS ON HIS PAINTINGS

MELANCHOLY AND HER COMPANIONS

These personifications are all brought together in this design, surrounding the Principal Figure Who is Melancholy Herself.

MILTON'S VISION OF THE MOON

Milton in his character of a Student at Cambridge, sees the Moon terrified as one led astray in the midst of her path thru heaven. The distant Steeple seen across a wide water indicates the sound of the Curfew Bell.

MILTON AND THE SPIRIT OF PLATO

The Spirit of Plato unfolds his Worlds to Milton in Contemplation. The Three Destinies sit on the Circles of Plato's Heavens, weaving the Thread of Mortal Life; these Heavens are Venus, Jupiter & Mars. Hermes flies before as attending on the Heaven of Jupiter; the Great Bear is seen in the sky beneath Hermes & the Spirits of Fire, Air, Water & Earth Surround Milton's Chair.

MILTON LED BY MELANCHOLY

Milton led by Melancholy into the Groves away from the Sun's flaming Beams, who is seen in the Heavens throwing his darts & flames of fire. The Spirits of the Trees on each side are seen under the domination of Insects raised by the Sun's heat.

MILTON'S DREAM

Milton Sleeping on a Bank; Sleep descending, with a strange, Mysterious dream upon his Wings, of Scrolls & Nets & Webs, unfolded by Spirits in the Air & in the Brook. Around Milton are Six Spirits or Fairies, hovering on the air, with Instruments of Music.

THE PEACEFUL HERMITAGE

Milton in his Old Age sitting in his "Mossy Cell," Contemplating the Constellations, surrounded by the Spirits of the Herbs & Flowers, bursts forth into a rapturous Prophetic Strain.

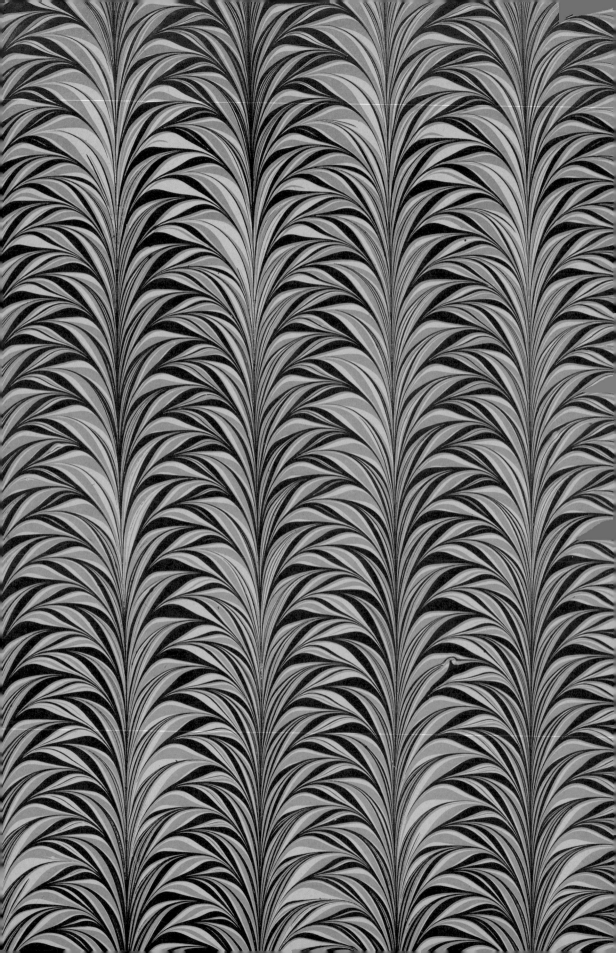